AF447489

Pet Breeding Profits: The Entrepreneur's Guide to Rabbit Sales

Copyright Page

TITLE: Pet Breeding Profits: The Entrepreneur's Guide to Rabbit Sales

1ST Edition

Copyright @ 2023

Roberto M. Rodriguez. All rights reserved.

ISBN: 9798223784036

Table of Contents

Pet Breeding Profits: The Entrepreneur's Guide to Rabbit Sales

By Roberto Miguel Rodriguez

Chapter 1: Introduction to Rabbit Breeding as a Profitable Venture

The Rise of the Rabbit Breeding Industry

In recent years, the rabbit breeding industry has experienced a remarkable surge in popularity, attracting entrepreneurs from various niches such as breeding and selling rare rabbit breeds, raising rabbits for meat production, rabbit fur farming and selling pelts, rabbit manure production for organic gardening, rabbit showmanship and competing in rabbit shows, rabbit pet breeding and sales, rabbit milk production for specialty products, rabbit therapy and emotional support rabbit breeding, rabbit breeding and sales for laboratory research, as well as rabbit agility training and competitions. This subchapter delves into the factors contributing to the rise of this industry and the lucrative opportunities it presents for aspiring entrepreneurs.

One of the key drivers behind the growing interest in rabbit breeding is the increasing demand for unique and rare rabbit breeds. With a rising number of enthusiasts and collectors, entrepreneurs specializing in breeding and selling these breeds have found a profitable niche market. The allure of owning a rare rabbit breed, often accompanied by higher price tags, has created a breeding frenzy among entrepreneurs looking to capitalize on this demand.

Another segment experiencing considerable growth is the rabbit meat production industry. As consumers become more health-conscious and seek alternative protein sources, rabbit meat has gained traction as a lean and sustainable option. Entrepreneurs involved in raising rabbits for meat production have tapped into this trend, offering high-quality, ethically-raised meat products to meet the growing demand.

Rabbit fur farming and selling pelts have also seen a resurgence in recent years. The fashion industry's shift towards sustainability and cruelty-free alternatives has led to an increased demand for rabbit fur. Entrepreneurs involved in this niche have recognized the opportunity to provide ethically-sourced fur products, catering to consumers who prioritize animal welfare and sustainable fashion.

Beyond the realms of fashion and food, rabbit manure production for organic gardening has become a profitable venture. Rabbit manure is highly sought after for its nutrient-rich composition, making it an ideal natural fertilizer. Entrepreneurs in this field have capitalized on the growing interest in organic gardening, offering sustainable and eco-friendly solutions to gardeners and farmers.

In addition to these niches, rabbit breeding and sales cater to various other industries such as laboratory research, rabbit therapy, emotional support breeding, and even rabbit agility training and competitions. These specialized areas offer unique opportunities for entrepreneurs to tap into untapped markets and provide tailored services to their target audiences.

As the rabbit breeding industry continues to thrive, entrepreneurs across these niches are finding success by capitalizing on the increasing demand for rare breeds, rabbit meat, fur, manure, therapy animals, and more. With careful planning, dedication, and a solid understanding of the target market, entrepreneurs in the rabbit breeding industry can achieve substantial profits while contributing to the growth and development of this flourishing industry.

Understanding the Potential Profitability of Rabbit Sales

Rabbit sales offer a lucrative opportunity for entrepreneurs in various niches, including breeding and selling rare rabbit breeds, raising rabbits for meat production, rabbit fur farming and selling pelts, rabbit manure production for organic gardening, rabbit showmanship and competing in rabbit shows, rabbit pet breeding and sales, rabbit milk production for specialty products, rabbit therapy and emotional support rabbit breeding, rabbit breeding and sales for laboratory research, and rabbit agility training and competitions. This subchapter aims to provide entrepreneurs in these niches with a comprehensive understanding of the potential profitability of rabbit sales.

Breeding and selling rare rabbit breeds can be a highly profitable venture. The demand for unique and rare rabbit breeds is constantly increasing. By carefully selecting and breeding specific breeds, entrepreneurs can command higher prices and attract a niche market of rabbit enthusiasts.

Raising rabbits for meat production is another profitable niche. With the rising demand for organic and locally sourced meat, entrepreneurs can tap into this market by providing high-quality rabbit meat. The low cost of production, fast growth rate, and high reproduction rate of rabbits make this niche highly profitable.

Rabbit fur farming and selling pelts offer entrepreneurs an opportunity to cater to the fashion and textile industries. The demand for rabbit fur remains strong, particularly in colder regions. By investing in proper breeding and fur processing techniques, entrepreneurs can generate substantial profits from selling rabbit pelts.

Rabbit manure production for organic gardening is a niche that appeals to environmentally conscious consumers. Rabbit manure is a rich source of organic nutrients and is highly sought after by gardeners. Entrepreneurs can capitalize on this demand by selling rabbit manure as a premium organic fertilizer.

Rabbit showmanship and competing in rabbit shows can be a profitable avenue for entrepreneurs who have a passion for rabbit breeding and showcasing their animals. By consistently producing high-quality rabbits that win awards, entrepreneurs can attract higher prices and establish a reputation within the rabbit showmanship community.

Rabbit pet breeding and sales offer entrepreneurs an opportunity to cater to the growing demand for companion animals. With their friendly nature and ease of care, rabbits make excellent pets. By breeding and selling well-socialized and healthy rabbits, entrepreneurs can generate substantial profits from this niche market.

Rabbit milk production for specialty products is a niche that appeals to consumers looking for alternative dairy products. Rabbit milk is highly nutritious and can be used to produce specialty products like cheese, soap, and cosmetics. Entrepreneurs can tap into this market by establishing rabbit milk production facilities and creating unique rabbit milk-based products.

Rabbit therapy and emotional support rabbit breeding offer entrepreneurs a chance to combine their love for rabbits with helping others. With the increasing recognition of the therapeutic benefits of animals, particularly rabbits, entrepreneurs can breed and sell rabbits specifically trained for therapy and emotional support purposes.

Rabbit breeding and sales for laboratory research is a niche that caters to the scientific and medical communities. By supplying research institutions with genetically diverse and well-maintained rabbit colonies, entrepreneurs can establish long-term contracts and ensure a steady income stream.

Rabbit agility training and competitions provide entrepreneurs with an opportunity to showcase the athletic abilities of rabbits and compete in various events. By training rabbits to navigate obstacle courses and participating in agility competitions, entrepreneurs can attract sponsorships, prize money, and build a reputation within the rabbit agility community.

In conclusion, the potential profitability of rabbit sales is vast and varied, offering entrepreneurs in breeding and selling rare rabbit breeds, raising rabbits for meat production, rabbit fur farming and selling pelts, rabbit manure production for organic gardening, rabbit showmanship and competing in rabbit shows, rabbit pet breeding and sales, rabbit milk production for specialty products, rabbit therapy and emotional support rabbit breeding, rabbit breeding and sales for laboratory research, and rabbit agility training and competitions ample opportunities to generate substantial profits. By understanding the unique dynamics of each niche and implementing effective business strategies, entrepreneurs can maximize their profitability and establish successful ventures in the rabbit sales industry.

Identifying the Target Market for Rare Rabbit Breeds

In the world of rabbit breeding, targeting the right market is crucial for the success of your business. When it comes to rare rabbit breeds, understanding your target market becomes even more important. In this subchapter, we will explore the various niches within the rabbit breeding industry and identify the potential buyers for these unique and sought-after breeds.

Breeding and selling rare rabbit breeds require a specific set of skills and knowledge. As an entrepreneur in this niche, your target market will consist of fellow breeders, enthusiasts, and collectors who have a passion for these special rabbits. These individuals often seek out rare breeds to add diversity and value to their existing breeding programs.

Raising rabbits for meat production is another niche within the industry. While rare rabbit breeds may not be the first choice for meat production, there is still a market for those who appreciate the unique taste and texture these breeds offer. Gourmet restaurants, specialty food stores, and individuals who prioritize quality and taste in their meat choices are potential customers for your rare rabbit breeds.

For those involved in rabbit fur farming and selling pelts, targeting high-end fashion designers, luxury boutiques, and fur enthusiasts will be essential. These individuals value the rarity and exclusivity that rare rabbit breeds can provide in their fur products.

Rabbit manure production for organic gardening is a growing trend, and eco-conscious gardeners are becoming more aware of the benefits of rabbit manure. Targeting organic farmers, garden centers, and environmentally-friendly consumers will help you tap into this market.

Rabbit showmanship and competing in rabbit shows is a popular hobby for many enthusiasts. Show breeders and participants are always on the lookout for unique and rare breeds that can give them an advantage in competitions. Targeting this market will require networking within the rabbit show community and participating in relevant events.

Rabbit pet breeding and sales is a niche that caters to individuals looking for companion animals. Certain rare rabbit breeds are highly sought after as pets due to their distinctive appearances, temperaments, or hypoallergenic qualities. Marketing to pet stores, online platforms, and directly to potential pet owners will help you reach this target market.

Rabbit milk production for specialty products is a niche that requires expertise and specialized facilities. Targeting gourmet food producers, artisanal cheese makers, and individuals with specific dietary needs can be profitable in this market.

Rabbit therapy and emotional support rabbit breeding is a niche that serves individuals in need of emotional support animals. Collaborating with therapists, hospitals, and support organizations can help you reach potential customers in this market.

Rabbit breeding and sales for laboratory research is a niche that requires compliance with strict regulations and ethical considerations.

Establishing partnerships with research institutions, universities, and pharmaceutical companies will be essential in targeting this market.

Lastly, rabbit agility training and competitions have gained popularity in recent years. Targeting rabbit agility clubs, trainers, and enthusiasts will help you connect with potential buyers of rare breeds that excel in agility competitions.

In conclusion, understanding the target market for rare rabbit breeds is crucial for success in the breeding and selling industry. By identifying the right market for your specific niche, you can effectively tailor your marketing efforts and maximize your profits as an entrepreneur in this field.

Chapter 2: Breeding and Selling Rare Rabbit Breeds

Selecting the Right Breeds for Profitable Sales

In the world of pet breeding, choosing the right breeds is crucial for ensuring profitable sales. Whether you are interested in breeding and selling rare rabbit breeds, raising rabbits for meat production, or engaging in rabbit fur farming, the success of your venture begins with selecting the right breeds. This subchapter will provide valuable insights and tips to help you make informed decisions when it comes to breed selection.

Breeding and selling rare rabbit breeds can be an exciting and lucrative niche. However, it requires careful consideration and research. Identify breeds that are in high demand and have unique characteristics that set them apart from common breeds. Consider factors such as rarity, appearance, temperament, and market demand. Engage with breeders and enthusiasts in the rabbit community to gain insights into which breeds are currently popular and have the potential for profitable sales.

For entrepreneurs interested in raising rabbits for meat production, selecting the right breeds is crucial to maximize profits. Look for breeds that are known for their meat quality, growth rate, and feed conversion efficiency. Popular meat rabbit breeds include New Zealand Whites, Californians, and Flemish Giants. Consider the local market demand and consumer preferences when making your selection.

Rabbit fur farming and selling pelts can be a niche with great profit potential. When choosing breeds for fur production, prioritize those with dense, luxurious fur that is in high demand. Breeds such as Rex and Angora rabbits are known for their soft and dense fur, making them desirable for pelts. However, keep in mind that fur farming may require additional knowledge and specialized care.

If you are interested in rabbit manure production for organic gardening, breeds that produce a large quantity of manure and have a balanced nutrient profile are ideal. Breeds like the Californian and New Zealand Whites are known for their prolific manure production, which can be a valuable resource for organic gardeners.

In the world of rabbit showmanship and competing in rabbit shows, breed selection is critical for success. Look for breeds that conform to the breed standards and have desirable features that judges look for. Participating in local rabbit shows and engaging with experienced show breeders can provide valuable guidance in breed selection for this niche.

For entrepreneurs interested in rabbit pet breeding and sales, selecting breeds that are known for their friendly temperament and adaptability to indoor living is essential. Popular pet breeds include the Dutch, Holland Lop, and Mini Rex. Ensure that the chosen breeds are in demand and have a reputation for being good companions for families and individuals.

Other niches, such as rabbit milk production for specialty products, rabbit therapy and emotional support rabbit breeding, rabbit breeding and sales for laboratory research, and rabbit agility training and competitions, require specific breed considerations. Research these niches thoroughly and consult with experts in the respective fields to determine the most suitable breeds for each venture.

In conclusion, selecting the right breeds is a crucial step in ensuring profitable sales in the diverse world of rabbit breeding. Consider factors such as market demand, unique characteristics, and specific niche requirements when making your breed selection. Engage with experts, attend industry events, and stay updated on market trends to make informed decisions and maximize your success as an entrepreneur in the rabbit breeding industry.

Establishing a Breeding Program for Rare Rabbit Breeds

In the world of rabbit breeding, there is a niche that offers immense opportunities for entrepreneurs – breeding and selling rare rabbit breeds. These unique and often hard-to-find breeds are highly sought after by enthusiasts, collectors, and even those looking for a new and interesting pet. If you have a passion for rabbits and want to turn it into a profitable venture, establishing a breeding program for rare rabbit breeds could be the perfect niche for you.

To begin, it is essential to research and identify the rare rabbit breeds that have a market demand. These breeds are typically characterized by their distinct physical features, unique coat colors, or specific genetic traits. Take the time to learn about their history, characteristics, and potential genetic issues to ensure you can provide the best care and breeding practices for these special breeds.

Next, you'll need to acquire high-quality breeding stock. Look for reputable breeders who specialize in rare rabbit breeds and are known for their healthy and well-cared-for animals. It's crucial to select rabbits with good genetic backgrounds and desirable traits to ensure the success of your breeding program.

Creating a suitable breeding environment is vital for the well-being and productivity of your rabbits. Provide spacious and clean enclosures with adequate ventilation, temperature control, and enrichment opportunities to ensure their physical and mental well-being. Regular veterinary check-ups and proper nutrition are also essential to maintain the health of your breeding stock.

Developing a breeding plan is crucial for achieving your goals. Consider factors such as the number of litters you aim to produce each year, the target market for each breed, and the pricing strategy you'll adopt. Additionally, you should establish a record-keeping system to track breeding pairings, birth dates, genetic information, and any other relevant data. This will enable you to make informed decisions and continuously improve your breeding program.

Marketing your rare rabbit breeds is the key to success in this niche. Utilize various channels such as social media, online marketplaces, breed-specific forums, and local rabbit shows to connect with potential buyers. Highlight the unique features and qualities of your rare breeds, emphasizing their scarcity and desirability. Building a strong network within the rabbit breeding community can also be beneficial for referrals and collaborations.

In conclusion, establishing a breeding program for rare rabbit breeds offers a promising opportunity for entrepreneurs passionate about rabbits. By conducting thorough research, acquiring high-quality breeding stock, creating a suitable breeding environment, developing a breeding plan, and implementing effective marketing strategies, you can turn your love for rabbits into a profitable venture. Remember, it takes dedication, patience, and continuous learning to succeed in this niche, but the rewards can be substantial.

Marketing and Selling Strategies for Rare Rabbit Breeds

Introduction:

Breeding and selling rare rabbit breeds can be a profitable venture for entrepreneurs looking to tap into various niche markets. This subchapter will provide valuable insights and strategies to effectively market and sell rare rabbit breeds to different target audiences. Whether you are focusing on rabbit fur farming, rabbit therapy breeding, or other niche markets, these strategies will help you maximize your profits and reach your business goals.

1. Understanding Your Target Audience:

To successfully market and sell rare rabbit breeds, it is crucial to understand the needs and preferences of your target audience. Conduct thorough market research to identify the specific niche markets you want to target, such as rabbit fur farming, organic gardening, or rabbit therapy breeding.

2. Developing a Unique Selling Proposition:

Differentiate your rare rabbit breeds from competitors by developing a unique selling proposition. Highlight the special characteristics, qualities, or benefits of your rabbits that set them apart from others in the market. This could include superior genetics, unique fur colors, or specific traits that make them ideal for certain purposes.

3. Building an Online Presence:

In today's digital age, having a strong online presence is vital for any business. Create a professional website and utilize social media platforms to promote your rare rabbit breeds. Share engaging content, high-quality photos, and videos that showcase the unique features and benefits of your rabbits. Engage with your audience through interactive posts, contests, and giveaways to build a loyal following.

4. Partnering with Influencers and Experts:

Collaborate with influencers and experts in the rabbit breeding industry to gain credibility and reach a wider audience. Seek endorsements from renowned breeders or experts who can vouch for the quality and uniqueness of your rare rabbit breeds. This can be done through partnerships, guest blog posts, or interviews, helping you establish your brand as a trusted authority in the market.

5. Participating in Trade Shows and Exhibitions:

Trade shows and exhibitions provide excellent opportunities to showcase your rare rabbit breeds to a targeted audience. Participate in relevant events, such as rabbit shows or fur farming expos, to network with potential buyers and breeders. Create visually appealing displays, offer product demonstrations, and provide informative brochures to leave a lasting impression on visitors.

Conclusion:

Marketing and selling rare rabbit breeds require a strategic approach tailored to specific niche markets. By understanding your target audience, creating a unique selling proposition, building an online presence, partnering with influencers, and participating in trade shows, you can effectively promote and sell your rare rabbit breeds to the right customers. Implement these strategies and watch your profits soar in the competitive world of rabbit breeding and sales.

Chapter 3: Raising Rabbits for Meat Production

Choosing Meat Breeds for Optimal Production

When it comes to breeding rabbits for meat production, selecting the right meat breeds is crucial for achieving optimal results. As an entrepreneur in the rabbit breeding industry, it is essential to understand the characteristics and qualities of different meat breeds to ensure a successful and profitable venture.

One of the most popular meat breeds is the New Zealand White. Known for their excellent meat-to-bone ratio and fast growth rate, New Zealand Whites are highly sought after by meat producers. Their large size and docile temperament make them easy to handle and manage, making them a favorite among novice breeders as well.

Another popular choice for meat production is the Californian breed. These rabbits have a striking appearance with their white bodies and distinctive black markings on their nose, ears, feet, and tail. Californians are known for their rapid growth and high meat quality, making them a top choice for commercial meat production.

For entrepreneurs interested in producing specialty meat products, the Flemish Giant breed is worth considering. These rabbits are the largest breed and can reach weights of up to 20 pounds. Their size makes them ideal for producing larger cuts of meat, such as roasts, and their meat is known for its tenderness and flavor.

When selecting meat breeds, it is essential to consider factors such as feed conversion efficiency, growth rate, and overall meat quality. Conducting thorough research and consulting with experienced breeders can provide valuable insights into which breeds are best suited for your specific goals and market demands.

In addition to breed selection, proper husbandry practices play a significant role in optimizing meat production. Providing a balanced diet, ample space, and regular health checks are essential for ensuring the overall well-being and growth of the rabbits.

As an entrepreneur in the rabbit meat production niche, it is crucial to stay updated on industry trends and consumer preferences. Being knowledgeable about different meat breeds and their qualities can give you a competitive edge in the market and help you meet the demands of your target audience.

In conclusion, choosing the right meat breeds for optimal production is a critical factor in the success of your rabbit breeding and meat production business. By selecting breeds that excel in growth rate, meat quality, and market demand, and implementing proper husbandry practices, you can ensure a profitable venture in the rabbit meat industry.

Setting Up a Profitable Meat Rabbit Operation

Introduction:

In this subchapter, we will explore the various aspects of setting up a profitable meat rabbit operation. If you are an entrepreneur looking to tap into the lucrative market of meat production, this guide will provide you with valuable insights and practical tips to maximize your success.

Choosing the Right Breeds:

To ensure a profitable venture, it is essential to select the right rabbit breeds for meat production. Some popular choices include New Zealand Whites, Californians, and Flemish Giants. These breeds are known for their fast growth rate, high meat-to-bone ratio, and excellent meat quality. Researching and understanding the specific traits of each breed will help you make an informed decision.

Housing and Infrastructure:

Creating a suitable housing environment is crucial for the well-being and productivity of your meat rabbits. Design and construct spacious and well-ventilated hutches that provide ample space for the rabbits to move around. Consider using wire cages to keep them safe from predators. Implement a proper waste management system to maintain cleanliness and prevent diseases.

Feeding and Nutrition:

A healthy and balanced diet plays a significant role in ensuring the growth and development of meat rabbits. Provide them with a constant supply of fresh water and a diet rich in fiber, protein, and essential nutrients. Consult with a veterinarian or a rabbit nutritionist to determine the appropriate feed ration for optimal growth and productivity.

Breeding and Reproduction:

Successful breeding is crucial for a profitable meat rabbit operation. Develop a breeding program that focuses on selecting the best breeding stock to enhance meat quality and growth rate. Implement proper mating techniques and ensure regular health check-ups to prevent any potential breeding issues. Consider implementing artificial insemination techniques to improve breeding efficiency.

Marketing and Sales:

Establishing a strong marketing strategy is essential to ensure the profitability of your meat rabbit operation. Identify your target market and tailor your marketing efforts accordingly. Utilize online platforms, social media, and local farmer's markets to promote your products. Highlight the unique selling points of your meat rabbits, such as their high-quality meat, organic upbringing, and sustainable farming practices.

Conclusion:

Setting up a profitable meat rabbit operation requires careful planning, knowledge, and dedication. By choosing the right breeds, providing suitable housing and nutrition, implementing effective breeding techniques, and adopting a robust marketing strategy, you can establish a successful venture in the meat rabbit industry. Remember to continuously educate yourself, stay updated with industry trends, and adapt your strategies to ensure long-term profitability.

Slaughtering and Processing Rabbits for Meat Sales

When it comes to running a successful rabbit breeding business, understanding the process of slaughtering and processing rabbits for meat sales is essential. This subchapter will provide you with valuable insights and tips on how to effectively handle this aspect of your entrepreneurial venture.

Breeding and selling rare rabbit breeds, raising rabbits for meat production, and rabbit fur farming and selling pelts are just a few niches within the rabbit industry that can benefit from learning about slaughtering and processing techniques.

First and foremost, it is crucial to prioritize the welfare of the rabbits throughout the entire process. As an entrepreneur in the rabbit industry, it is your responsibility to ensure that ethical and humane practices are followed. This includes providing a stress-free and comfortable environment for the rabbits leading up to the slaughter.

When it comes to the actual slaughter, it is important to have the necessary equipment and knowledge to do it efficiently and humanely. This may involve using a specialized knife or a mechanical device specifically designed for rabbit slaughtering. The aim is to minimize stress and pain for the animal.

After the slaughter, the processing phase begins. This involves skinning, evisceration, and butchering the meat. For entrepreneurs involved in rabbit fur farming, this step is crucial in preparing the pelts for sale. Proper skinning techniques will ensure the quality and value of the fur.

Entrepreneurs specializing in meat production should be knowledgeable about different cuts of rabbit meat and how to package and store them properly. This will ensure that the meat remains fresh and safe for consumption.

Additionally, entrepreneurs interested in rabbit manure production for organic gardening can also benefit from proper slaughtering and processing techniques. By efficiently utilizing the byproducts of the slaughter, such as the rabbit offal, entrepreneurs can generate organic fertilizer for their gardening endeavors.

It is important to note that regulations and guidelines surrounding the slaughtering and processing of rabbits may vary depending on your location. Familiarize yourself with the local laws and regulations to ensure compliance.

Regardless of your niche within the rabbit industry, understanding the process of slaughtering and processing rabbits for meat sales is crucial for success. By prioritizing the welfare of the animals and following ethical practices, you can ensure the quality of your products and build a reputable brand within the market.

Chapter 4: Rabbit Fur Farming and Selling Pelts

Understanding the Market Demand for Rabbit Pelts

In the world of pet breeding, there are numerous avenues for entrepreneurs to explore and profit from. One such niche that has gained popularity in recent years is rabbit fur farming and selling pelts. This subchapter aims to provide valuable insights into understanding the market demand for rabbit pelts, equipping entrepreneurs with the necessary knowledge to tap into this profitable business opportunity.

Breeding and selling rare rabbit breeds, raising rabbits for meat production, and even rabbit manure production for organic gardening have their own unique niches in the pet breeding industry. However, rabbit fur farming and selling pelts offer an entirely different avenue for entrepreneurs looking to capitalize on the growing demand for fur products.

Rabbit pelts are highly sought after for their softness, warmth, and versatility. They are often used for making luxurious garments, accessories, and home decor items. With a rising focus on sustainable and ethical fashion, rabbit fur has gained prominence as a cruelty-free alternative to other fur types.

To understand the market demand for rabbit pelts, it is crucial to research and identify key factors that influence consumer preferences. These factors include fashion trends, consumer demographics, and the availability of other fur alternatives in the market. By staying updated on the latest fashion trends and consumer preferences, entrepreneurs can tailor their breeding and selling strategies to meet the market demand.

Additionally, collaborating with fashion designers, retailers, and artisans can help entrepreneurs establish a strong foothold in the rabbit fur market. Building relationships with these stakeholders can lead to lucrative partnerships and increased exposure for rabbit pelts.

Entrepreneurs venturing into the rabbit fur farming and pelt selling industry should also consider the legal and ethical implications of their business. Adhering to animal welfare standards and ensuring sustainable breeding practices will not only attract conscious consumers but also safeguard the reputation and longevity of the business.

Understanding the market demand for rabbit pelts is essential for entrepreneurs looking to enter the fur farming and pelt selling industry. By staying informed about consumer preferences, building strategic partnerships, and adhering to ethical practices, entrepreneurs can tap into this lucrative market and maximize their profits. With the right knowledge and approach, rabbit fur farming and selling pelts can become a thriving business opportunity within the broader pet breeding industry.

Establishing a Fur Farming Operation

Fur farming has emerged as a lucrative niche within the pet breeding industry, offering entrepreneurs a unique opportunity to profit from the demand for high-quality rabbit pelts. If you are looking to venture into fur farming, this subchapter will guide you through the process of establishing a successful fur farming operation.

First and foremost, it is crucial to select the right rabbit breeds for fur production. Breeds such as Angora, Rex, and Satin are known for their luxurious fur, making them highly sought after in the market. Conduct thorough research to identify the breeds that are in high demand and align with your business goals.

Next, you need to create suitable housing facilities for your rabbits. Fur farming requires spacious and well-designed hutches that provide optimal comfort and protection. Ensure that the hutches are properly ventilated, insulated, and predator-proof. Additionally, invest in proper lighting systems to facilitate the natural growth of fur.

Feeding your rabbits a balanced and nutritious diet is essential for their overall health and the quality of their fur. Consult with a veterinarian or a rabbit nutritionist to develop a feeding regimen that meets the specific nutritional requirements of fur-producing rabbits. High-quality forage, pellets, and supplements should be included in their diet.

To maintain the optimal coat quality, regular grooming and care are essential. Establish a grooming routine that includes regular brushing, bathing, and trimming to prevent matting and tangling of the fur. This will ensure that your pelts are in excellent condition and fetch higher prices in the market.

Marketing and selling your rabbit pelts is a crucial aspect of establishing a fur farming operation. Identify potential buyers such as furriers, fashion designers, and craft enthusiasts. Attend trade shows, exhibitions, and networking events to showcase your pelts and build valuable connections within the industry.

Additionally, consider diversifying your revenue streams by exploring other fur-related products. This could include selling rabbit fur accessories like hats, gloves, and scarves, or collaborating with local artisans to create unique fur-based crafts.

Remember, fur farming requires a strong commitment to animal welfare and ethical practices. Ensure that your rabbits are well-cared for, receive regular veterinary check-ups, and have access to clean water and a comfortable environment.

By following these guidelines and continuously learning about the industry trends, you can establish a successful fur farming operation that caters to the niche market of rabbit fur enthusiasts. With dedication and passion, your fur farm can become a profitable venture in the pet breeding industry.

Harvesting and Processing Rabbit Pelts for Sale

Rabbit fur farming is an increasingly popular niche in the world of entrepreneurship, with the demand for rabbit pelts on the rise. In this subchapter, we will explore the process of harvesting and processing rabbit pelts for sale, providing valuable insights for entrepreneurs who are interested in tapping into the lucrative rabbit fur market.

First and foremost, it is essential to breed and raise rabbits specifically for their fur. Breeding and selling rare rabbit breeds can be a viable option, as unique fur patterns and colors tend to fetch higher prices in the market. Selecting rabbits with thick, dense, and high-quality fur is crucial to ensure the profitability of your venture.

Once the rabbits have reached maturity, it is time to harvest their pelts. This process should be carried out with utmost care and precision to ensure the fur remains intact and undamaged. Expertise in skinning techniques is vital to maintain the value of the pelts. It is recommended to seek guidance from experienced furriers or fur farming associations to learn the best practices for skinning rabbits.

After the pelts have been harvested, they need to be processed to transform them into market-ready products. This involves removing any remaining flesh, fat, or membrane from the hides. The hides are then carefully washed and dried to remove moisture and prevent any potential issues such as mold or decay.

The next step is tanning the pelts, a crucial process that enhances their durability and overall quality. Entrepreneurs can choose from various tanning methods, including traditional methods using natural substances like tree barks or modern methods utilizing synthetic chemicals. Understanding the tanning process and its impact on the final product is essential to produce high-quality rabbit pelts that meet market demands.

Finally, entrepreneurs must market and sell their rabbit pelts effectively. Building a network of potential buyers, such as furriers, fashion designers, or retailers, is crucial to establish a steady customer base. Utilizing online platforms, attending trade shows, or even collaborating with other entrepreneurs in related niches can greatly enhance your visibility in the market.

In conclusion, harvesting and processing rabbit pelts for sale can be a profitable venture for entrepreneurs interested in the fur farming industry. By breeding and raising rabbits specifically for their fur, mastering the art of skinning, processing, and tanning pelts, and effectively marketing their products, entrepreneurs can tap into the growing demand for rabbit pelts and establish a successful business in this niche market.

Chapter 5: Rabbit Manure Production for Organic Gardening

Utilizing Rabbit Manure as Organic Fertilizer

In the world of rabbit breeding, there is more to profit than just selling rabbits. As an entrepreneur in the various niches of the rabbit industry, it is essential to explore all avenues to maximize your earnings. One such opportunity lies in utilizing rabbit manure as organic fertilizer, a practice that not only benefits your garden but also contributes to sustainable and eco-friendly practices.

Rabbit manure is a nutrient-rich organic material that can greatly enhance the health and productivity of your plants. Unlike synthetic fertilizers, rabbit manure is completely natural and free from harmful chemicals, making it ideal for organic gardening. The high levels of nitrogen, phosphorus, and potassium found in rabbit manure promote healthy plant growth, increase yields, and improve soil structure.

To start utilizing rabbit manure as organic fertilizer, you need to establish a system for collecting and composting it. One option is to create a designated manure pile or compost bin in your rabbitry. Regularly clean the rabbit cages, removing the soiled bedding and droppings, and add them to the compost pile. Ensure that the manure is mixed with other organic materials, such as straw or leaves, to create a balanced and nutritious compost.

Once you have a sufficient amount of compost, it is time to apply it to your garden. Spread a layer of compost around the base of your plants, taking care not to pile it up against the stems. Alternatively, you can mix the compost with soil before planting to provide a nutrient-rich environment for your crops.

Not only does utilizing rabbit manure as organic fertilizer benefit your garden, but it also offers a sustainable waste management solution for your rabbitry. By converting the manure into compost, you reduce the amount of waste generated and minimize the risk of pollution.

As an entrepreneur in the breeding and selling of rare rabbit breeds, raising rabbits for meat production, or even rabbit fur farming and selling pelts, incorporating the use of rabbit manure as organic fertilizer can provide an additional stream of income. Package and market your compost as a premium organic fertilizer, catering to the growing demand for sustainable and environmentally friendly gardening practices.

In conclusion, harnessing the power of rabbit manure as organic fertilizer can significantly benefit both your garden and your business. By implementing sustainable practices, you not only contribute to a healthier environment but also tap into a niche market that values organic and eco-friendly products. So, go ahead and turn your rabbit manure into a valuable resource that will not only boost your profits but also promote sustainable agriculture.

Creating a Rabbit Manure Production System

Introduction:

In this subchapter, we will explore the potential of rabbit manure as a valuable resource for entrepreneurs engaged in various rabbit-related niches. Whether you are breeding and selling rare rabbit breeds, raising rabbits for meat production, or involved in any other rabbit-related business, implementing a rabbit manure production system can significantly enhance your profitability and sustainability. Rabbit manure is a nutrient-rich organic fertilizer that can be used in organic gardening, horticulture, and even specialty product manufacturing. Let's dive into the details of creating an efficient rabbit manure production system.

Benefits of Rabbit Manure:

Rabbit manure is often referred to as "black gold" in the gardening world due to its numerous benefits. It is rich in essential nutrients such as nitrogen, phosphorus, and potassium, making it an excellent organic fertilizer. Unlike some other types of manure, rabbit manure does not need to be composted before use, which saves time and effort. Additionally, rabbit manure does not have a strong odor, making it more pleasant to work with compared to manure from larger animals.

Setting Up a Rabbit Manure Production System:

To establish a successful rabbit manure production system, you need to consider a few key factors:

1. Housing and Waste Management: Ensure that your rabbit housing is designed to collect manure efficiently. Consider using slatted floors or trays beneath the cages to capture droppings. Regular cleaning and waste management practices are essential to maintain a healthy and productive system.

2. Storage and Composting: Create a designated area for storing and composting rabbit manure. Composting helps break down the manure, making it even more beneficial for plants. Proper composting techniques, such as turning the pile regularly, will accelerate the decomposition process.

3. Marketing and Sales: Once you have a substantial amount of rabbit manure, explore potential markets for your product. Organic gardeners, horticulturists, and specialty product manufacturers are excellent target customers. Develop a marketing strategy to reach out to potential buyers and highlight the benefits of using rabbit manure.

4. Packaging and Distribution: Consider packaging options that are convenient for customers, such as bags, containers, or bulk deliveries.

Ensure that your distribution network is reliable and efficient, allowing you to deliver the rabbit manure promptly and in good condition.

Conclusion:

Implementing a rabbit manure production system can significantly boost your profitability and sustainability as an entrepreneur in the rabbit industry. By harnessing the nutrient-rich potential of rabbit manure, you can cater to various niches such as organic gardening, specialty product manufacturing, and more. Remember to focus on efficient waste management, composting, and marketing to ensure the success of your rabbit manure production system.

Marketing Rabbit Manure to Organic Gardeners

Introduction:

In today's eco-conscious world, organic gardening has gained immense popularity. Organic gardeners are constantly on the lookout for natural fertilizers that can enhance the health and productivity of their plants. One such highly effective and sustainable option is rabbit manure. This subchapter explores the potential of marketing rabbit manure to organic gardeners, providing entrepreneurs with an opportunity to tap into this profitable niche market.

Understanding the Market:

Organic gardeners prioritize using natural and sustainable products to nourish their plants. They are willing to pay a premium for high-quality organic fertilizers that promote soil health and enhance plant growth. Rabbit manure ticks all the boxes, containing essential nutrients like nitrogen, phosphorus, and potassium, as well as beneficial microorganisms that improve soil structure and fertility.

Benefits of Rabbit Manure:

Entrepreneurs entering the rabbit manure market must understand the unique selling points of this organic fertilizer. Rabbit manure is odorless, making it convenient for indoor gardening. It is also a cold manure, meaning it doesn't need composting before application. Additionally, due to the rabbit's herbivorous diet, the manure is weed-free, eliminating the risk of introducing unwanted seeds into gardens.

Developing a Marketing Strategy:

To succeed in marketing rabbit manure to organic gardeners, entrepreneurs should focus on the following strategies:

1. Product Packaging and Branding:

Create visually appealing packaging that highlights the organic and sustainable qualities of rabbit manure. Emphasize its benefits and its compatibility with organic gardening practices. Develop a memorable brand that resonates with the target audience.

2. Online Presence:

Establish a strong online presence through a dedicated website, social media platforms, and online marketplaces. Share valuable content, such as gardening tips and success stories, to build trust and engage with potential customers.

3. Local Partnerships:

Collaborate with local organic gardening stores, community gardens, and farmer's markets to showcase and sell rabbit manure. Offer educational workshops and demonstrations to raise awareness about the benefits of using rabbit manure.

4. Testimonials and Reviews:

Encourage satisfied customers to share their positive experiences and testimonials. These reviews can be featured on the website, social media, and promotional materials to boost credibility and attract new customers.

5. Sustainable Practices:

Highlight the eco-friendly nature of rabbit manure production, emphasizing the responsible breeding and welfare of rabbits. Educate customers about the positive environmental impact of using this natural fertilizer.

Conclusion:

Marketing rabbit manure to organic gardeners presents a lucrative opportunity for entrepreneurs in the rabbit breeding industry. By understanding the needs of the target market and developing effective marketing strategies, entrepreneurs can tap into this niche market and offer a sustainable and highly sought-after product. With the right approach, entrepreneurs can not only generate profits but also contribute to the growing demand for organic and eco-friendly gardening practices.

Chapter 6: Rabbit Showmanship and Competing in Rabbit Shows

Participating in Rabbit Shows for Recognition and Sales

For entrepreneurs involved in the breeding and selling of rare rabbit breeds, participating in rabbit shows can provide not only recognition but also a boost in sales. Rabbit shows are not only a platform for showcasing your exceptional breeds but also an opportunity to network with potential buyers, fellow breeders, and industry experts. This subchapter will guide you through the process of participating in rabbit shows, highlighting the benefits and strategies to maximize your success.

Recognition is crucial in the competitive world of rabbit breeding. Rabbit shows offer a platform where breeders can exhibit their unique breeds, gain exposure, and build a reputation for producing high-quality rabbits. By participating in shows and winning awards, you can establish yourself as a reputable breeder, which will attract potential buyers and increase sales.

Networking is another significant advantage of rabbit shows. These events bring together enthusiasts, breeders, and industry experts, creating an ideal environment for collaboration and knowledge-sharing. By engaging with others in the field, you can learn new techniques, stay updated on industry trends, and even find potential buyers or partners for future ventures.

To make the most of your participation in rabbit shows, it's essential to prepare thoroughly. This includes selecting and grooming your rabbits to showcase their best qualities, familiarizing yourself with the show's rules and regulations, and having all necessary paperwork in order. Additionally, consider creating promotional materials such as brochures or business cards to hand out to potential customers and contacts.

While recognition and networking are the primary goals of participating in rabbit shows, they can also directly impact your sales. Winning awards or receiving recognition from judges can significantly increase the perceived value of your rabbits, allowing you to command higher prices and attract more discerning customers. Additionally, the connections you make at these events can lead to direct sales or referrals, further boosting your business.

In conclusion, participating in rabbit shows is a valuable strategy for entrepreneurs in the rabbit breeding and sales industry. These shows offer recognition, networking opportunities, and a platform to showcase your rare breeds to potential buyers. By preparing thoroughly and leveraging the benefits of these events, you can elevate your business and increase sales in this niche market.

Training and Grooming Techniques for Show Rabbits

As an entrepreneur in the world of rabbit breeding and sales, it is essential to understand the importance of training and grooming techniques for show rabbits. Show rabbits are a special breed that requires extra care and attention to ensure they are in top condition for competitions. In this subchapter, we will explore the various techniques that can be used to train and groom show rabbits, helping you enhance their appearance and increase their chances of success in the show ring.

Grooming is a crucial aspect of preparing show rabbits for competitions. Regular brushing and combing help to keep their fur clean, smooth, and free from mats. It is important to invest in high-quality grooming tools, such as slicker brushes and grooming combs, to ensure the best results. Additionally, trimming the rabbit's nails regularly is necessary to prevent discomfort and potential injuries.

Bathing show rabbits is another vital grooming technique. However, it is important to note that rabbits are sensitive to water and may become stressed during the bathing process. Use lukewarm water and a gentle rabbit-specific shampoo to avoid irritating their skin. After bathing, thoroughly dry the rabbit using a towel or a hairdryer set on low heat to prevent them from catching a chill.

Training show rabbits involves teaching them specific skills and behaviors that will impress judges in the show ring. One of the most important skills is posing, where the rabbit stands still in a specific position, showcasing its best features. Start by using treats to encourage the rabbit to stand on a grooming table and gradually introduce the desired pose. Practice this regularly to ensure the rabbit becomes comfortable and confident in its pose.

Additionally, training show rabbits to walk on a leash is beneficial for mobility during competitions. Begin by introducing the rabbit to a harness and leash in a calm and controlled environment. Gradually increase the distance and duration of the walks, rewarding the rabbit with treats for good behavior. Remember to use a lightweight and comfortable harness specifically designed for rabbits.

In conclusion, training and grooming techniques are essential for preparing show rabbits for competitions. By investing time and effort into grooming their fur, trimming their nails, and bathing them regularly, you can enhance their appearance and overall presentation. Training them to pose and walk on a leash will also impress judges and increase their chances of success in the show ring. Remember to be patient and consistent with your training efforts, and always prioritize the comfort and well-being of your show rabbits.

Networking and Building a Reputation in the Rabbit Show Circuit

In the world of rabbit breeding and sales, building a reputation and establishing a strong network in the rabbit show circuit is crucial for success. As an entrepreneur in this industry, it is essential to understand the importance of networking and how it can positively impact your business and profitability.

Networking within the rabbit show circuit allows you to connect with other breeders, enthusiasts, and potential customers. By attending rabbit shows, participating in competitions, and actively engaging with others in the industry, you can create valuable relationships that can open doors to new opportunities and collaborations.

One of the primary benefits of networking is the exchange of knowledge and expertise. Connecting with experienced breeders and show competitors can provide you with invaluable insights into breeding techniques, showmanship, and general best practices. This knowledge can help you improve your own breeding program, enhance the quality of your rabbits, and increase your chances of success in the show ring.

Furthermore, networking allows you to showcase your own rabbits and gain recognition within the industry. By consistently participating in rabbit shows, you can build a reputation as a reputable breeder, known for producing high-quality and rare rabbit breeds. This positive reputation can attract potential buyers, sponsors, and even potential business partners.

Networking can also lead to business collaborations and joint ventures. By connecting with other entrepreneurs in related niches such as rabbit fur farming, rabbit manure production, or rabbit therapy breeding, you can explore opportunities for cross-promotion or mutually beneficial partnerships. For example, partnering with a rabbit fur farmer can lead to the sale of pelts from your rare rabbit breeds, generating additional revenue streams for your business.

To effectively network within the rabbit show circuit, it is essential to be proactive and engage with others both online and offline. Join online forums and social media groups dedicated to rabbit breeding and showmanship, attend local and national rabbit shows, and actively participate in workshops and seminars. Be open to learning from others, sharing your own experiences, and building genuine relationships within the industry.

In conclusion, networking and building a reputation in the rabbit show circuit is a vital component of success for entrepreneurs in the rabbit breeding and sales industry. By actively engaging with others, exchanging knowledge, showcasing your rabbits, and exploring collaborations, you can enhance your business, increase your profitability, and establish yourself as a respected figure within the industry.

Chapter 7: Rabbit Pet Breeding and Sales

Understanding the Pet Rabbit Market

The pet rabbit market is a thriving industry that offers numerous opportunities for entrepreneurs in various niches. Whether you are interested in breeding and selling rare rabbit breeds, raising rabbits for meat production, or even rabbit fur farming, this subchapter will provide you with valuable insights into the dynamics of the pet rabbit market.

One of the most popular niches in the pet rabbit market is breeding and selling rare rabbit breeds. With a growing demand for unique and exotic rabbit species, entrepreneurs can capitalize on this trend by offering exclusive breeds to enthusiasts and collectors. This subchapter will guide you through the process of identifying rare rabbit breeds, understanding their characteristics, and implementing effective marketing strategies to reach potential customers.

Another lucrative niche within the pet rabbit market is raising rabbits for meat production. With an increasing interest in sustainable and ethically sourced meat, entrepreneurs can tap into the demand for high-quality rabbit meat. This section will explore the best practices for raising rabbits for meat, including breeding, feeding, and processing. It will also provide insights into marketing strategies that target health-conscious consumers and gourmet restaurants.

For those interested in the fashion industry, rabbit fur farming and selling pelts can be a profitable venture. This subchapter will delve into the regulations and ethical considerations surrounding fur farming, as well as the techniques for breeding rabbits with desirable fur qualities. It will also explore the different markets for rabbit fur products, such as the fashion industry and craft enthusiasts.

In addition to the traditional markets, the pet rabbit industry offers unique niches such as rabbit manure production for organic gardening, rabbit showmanship and competing in rabbit shows, rabbit milk production for specialty products, rabbit therapy and emotional support rabbit breeding, rabbit breeding and sales for laboratory research, and rabbit agility training and competitions. Each of these niches presents distinct opportunities for entrepreneurs, and this subchapter will provide a comprehensive overview of their respective markets, including potential customers, marketing strategies, and industry trends.

By understanding the dynamics of the pet rabbit market, entrepreneurs can make informed decisions about which niches to pursue and how to best position their businesses for success. Whether you are passionate about breeding and selling rare rabbit breeds or interested in exploring the emerging markets of rabbit therapy or agility training, this subchapter will equip you with the knowledge and insights necessary to thrive in the pet rabbit industry.

Establishing a Successful Pet Breeding Program

Breeding and selling rare rabbit breeds, raising rabbits for meat production, rabbit fur farming and selling pelts, rabbit manure production for organic gardening, rabbit showmanship and competing in rabbit shows, rabbit pet breeding and sales, rabbit milk production for specialty products, rabbit therapy and emotional support rabbit breeding, rabbit breeding and sales for laboratory research, rabbit agility training and competitions.

Introduction:

A successful pet breeding program requires careful planning, dedication, and a deep understanding of the specific niche you intend to serve. Whether you are interested in breeding rare rabbit breeds, raising rabbits for meat production, or any other niche within the rabbit industry, this subchapter will provide you with valuable insights and strategies to establish and grow a profitable business.

1. Research and Select a Profitable Niche:

To ensure success, it is important to identify a niche within the rabbit industry that aligns with your interests and has a strong market demand. Conduct thorough research to understand the specific requirements, challenges, and potential profitability of your chosen niche.

2. Build a Strong Foundation:

Establishing a successful pet breeding program starts with a solid foundation. This includes acquiring high-quality breeding stock, ensuring proper housing and facilities, and implementing a comprehensive breeding plan. Consider partnering with experienced breeders, veterinarians, and industry experts to gain valuable insights and guidance.

3. Develop a Breeding Strategy:

Create a breeding strategy tailored to your niche. This includes understanding breeding cycles, selecting appropriate breeding pairs, and managing breeding records. Additionally, consider factors such as genetics, health, and temperament to produce high-quality offspring that meet the specific needs and demands of your target market.

4. Implement Effective Marketing Strategies:

To maximize your profitability, it is crucial to effectively market your rabbits and their associated products or services. Leverage online platforms, social media, and targeted advertising to reach your target audience. Establish a strong brand identity, showcase the unique qualities of your rabbits, and highlight any certifications or accolades that set your breeding program apart from competitors.

5. Provide Exceptional Customer Service:

Customer satisfaction is key to the success of your pet breeding program. Ensure prompt and professional communication, offer support and guidance to customers, and provide ongoing education on rabbit care and management. Building strong relationships with your customers will not only result in repeat business but also positive word-of-mouth referrals.

6. Continuously Improve and Adapt:

The rabbit industry is constantly evolving, and it is important to stay abreast of new trends, technologies, and industry standards. Attend industry conferences, join relevant associations, and network with other breeders to stay informed and continuously improve your breeding program.

Conclusion:

Establishing a successful pet breeding program requires dedication, knowledge, and a customer-focused approach. By understanding your chosen niche, implementing effective breeding and marketing strategies, and providing exceptional customer service, you can create a profitable and sustainable business in the rabbit industry.

Marketing and Selling Pet Rabbits

When it comes to the world of pet breeding and sales, rabbits are a popular choice for many entrepreneurs seeking to profit from their passion for animals. Whether you are interested in breeding and selling rare rabbit breeds, raising rabbits for meat production, or even rabbit fur farming and selling pelts, this subchapter will guide you through the intricacies of marketing and selling pet rabbits.

First and foremost, it is crucial to understand your target audience. Depending on your niche, you may be catering to various markets, such as rabbit show enthusiasts, organic gardeners in need of rabbit manure, or individuals seeking emotional support rabbits. Knowing your audience will help you tailor your marketing efforts to reach the right customers.

One of the most effective marketing strategies for selling pet rabbits is building a strong online presence. Create a website or social media accounts dedicated to showcasing your rabbits, their unique traits, and the benefits they offer. High-quality photographs, informative descriptions, and customer testimonials can help build credibility and attract potential buyers.

Additionally, consider participating in rabbit shows or competitions relevant to your niche. This not only gives you an opportunity to showcase your rabbits' qualities but also allows you to network with fellow breeders and potential customers. Word-of-mouth recommendations within the rabbit community can be invaluable for your business.

In order to maximize your sales potential, consider offering additional products or services. For instance, if you specialize in breeding rare rabbit breeds, you could also offer rabbit milk for specialty products or provide rabbit agility training and competitions. Diversifying your offerings can attract a wider customer base and increase revenue streams.

When it comes to selling pet rabbits, providing excellent customer service is key. Respond promptly to inquiries, be transparent about the rabbits' health and lineage, and offer post-purchase support and advice. Building strong relationships with your customers will not only increase the likelihood of repeat purchases but also lead to positive word-of-mouth referrals.

In conclusion, marketing and selling pet rabbits can be a rewarding entrepreneurial endeavor. By understanding your target audience, building an online presence, participating in relevant events, diversifying your offerings, and providing excellent customer service, you can establish a successful and profitable business in the world of pet breeding and sales.

Chapter 8: Rabbit Milk Production for Specialty Products

Exploring the Niche Market for Rabbit Milk Products

The world of rabbit breeding and sales offers a myriad of opportunities for entrepreneurs to capitalize on various niches. One such niche that has seen a surge in popularity in recent years is rabbit milk production for specialty products. With the rising demand for alternative dairy products and the increasing interest in unique and exotic ingredients, rabbit milk products have carved a unique space in the market.

Rabbit milk is known for its exceptional nutritional value, containing high levels of protein, vitamins, and minerals. It is also naturally low in cholesterol and fat, making it an attractive option for health-conscious consumers. Furthermore, rabbit milk is hypoallergenic, making it suitable for individuals with lactose intolerance or milk allergies.

Entrepreneurs interested in this niche can explore a range of rabbit milk-based products, including artisanal cheeses, skincare products, and nutritional supplements. The versatility of rabbit milk allows for a wide range of possibilities, catering to different customer preferences and dietary requirements.

To tap into the market for rabbit milk products, entrepreneurs need to establish a reliable and sustainable source of rabbit milk. This requires a well-planned breeding program that focuses on selecting rabbits with high milk production capabilities. Breeding and selling rare rabbit breeds that are known for their milk production potential can be a profitable endeavor.

In addition to breeding rabbits specifically for milk production, entrepreneurs can also consider utilizing existing rabbit populations involved in other niches, such as pet breeding and sales. By offering incentives to rabbit breeders, such as purchasing excess milk or partnering in a profit-sharing arrangement, entrepreneurs can create a mutually beneficial relationship that supports both industries.

Marketing and branding are crucial for success in the rabbit milk product market. Entrepreneurs should emphasize the unique qualities of rabbit milk, highlighting its health benefits, sustainability, and ethical production practices. Collaborating with local farmers' markets, health food stores, and specialty food retailers can help raise awareness and reach target consumers.

In conclusion, the niche market for rabbit milk products presents a promising opportunity for entrepreneurs in the rabbit breeding and sales industry. By focusing on breeding rabbits for milk production, developing a range of rabbit milk-based products, and implementing effective marketing strategies, entrepreneurs can tap into this growing market and establish a profitable business.

Implementing a Rabbit Milk Production System

As an entrepreneur in the rabbit breeding industry, you may have explored various avenues for generating profits, such as selling rare rabbit breeds, raising rabbits for meat production, or even venturing into rabbit fur farming. However, there is another niche that holds immense potential - rabbit milk production for specialty products.

Rabbit milk, although lesser-known compared to cow or goat milk, is gaining popularity among health-conscious consumers who are constantly seeking alternative and nutritious dairy options. This presents an opportunity for entrepreneurs to tap into a unique market and create a sustainable business model.

To successfully implement a rabbit milk production system, there are several key components to consider. Firstly, you need to carefully select the right rabbit breeds that are known for their milk-producing capabilities. Breeds such as the Blanc de Hotot or the American Sable are known to have high milk yields and could serve as an excellent foundation for your venture.

Next, you must establish a suitable infrastructure for housing and caring for the rabbits. This includes providing clean and spacious cages, ensuring proper ventilation, and maintaining optimal temperature and lighting conditions. It is crucial to prioritize the welfare and health of the rabbits to ensure the quality and quantity of milk production.

Feeding the rabbits a balanced diet is vital for milk production. Consult with a veterinarian or a rabbit nutrition specialist to develop a proper feeding regimen that includes a combination of high-quality hay, fresh vegetables, and specially-formulated pellets. Additionally, ensure a constant supply of clean water to keep the rabbits hydrated and promote milk production.

Milking the rabbits requires skill and expertise. Proper training and equipment are essential to ensure a hygienic and efficient milking process. It is imperative to adhere to strict sanitation protocols to prevent contamination and maintain the quality of the milk.

Once you have successfully implemented the rabbit milk production system, you can explore various avenues for selling your specialty products. Consider partnering with local health food stores, farmers' markets, or even online platforms that cater to niche dairy products. Promote the unique nutritional benefits of rabbit milk, such as its high protein and low cholesterol content, to attract health-conscious consumers.

With the right approach and dedication, implementing a rabbit milk production system can be a profitable venture within the rabbit breeding industry. By catering to the growing demand for alternative dairy products, you can carve out a unique niche for yourself as an entrepreneur in this field.

Developing and Marketing Rabbit Milk Specialty Products

Rabbit milk is a highly nutritious and lesser-known alternative to traditional dairy products. With its unique composition and potential health benefits, there is a growing demand for rabbit milk specialty products in the market. In this subchapter, we will explore the various aspects of developing and marketing these products to cater to the needs of entrepreneurs in different niches.

For entrepreneurs involved in breeding and selling rare rabbit breeds, incorporating rabbit milk specialty products into their offerings can be a lucrative addition. By highlighting the exceptional qualities of rabbit milk and its potential benefits, breeders can attract customers who are looking for unique and high-quality products.

Similarly, entrepreneurs in the niche of raising rabbits for meat production can diversify their product range by introducing rabbit milk specialty products. This can help them tap into a niche market and differentiate themselves from competitors while tapping into the health-conscious consumer base.

Entrepreneurs engaged in rabbit fur farming and selling pelts can leverage rabbit milk as an additional revenue stream. By developing rabbit milk-based skincare products, they can cater to a niche market that values natural and sustainable ingredients.

For entrepreneurs involved in rabbit manure production for organic gardening, rabbit milk can be marketed as a natural and nutrient-rich fertilizer. By highlighting its unique properties, such as its high nitrogen content and absence of harmful chemicals, entrepreneurs can attract environmentally-conscious gardeners.

Rabbit milk can also be used in the niche of rabbit showmanship and competing in rabbit shows. By developing rabbit milk-based treats and supplements, entrepreneurs can cater to the specific dietary requirements of show rabbits, enhancing their performance and overall health.

Additionally, entrepreneurs in the niche of rabbit pet breeding and sales can offer rabbit milk specialty products as a value-added service. By educating pet owners about the benefits of rabbit milk and providing them with easy access to these products, they can strengthen customer loyalty and generate additional revenue.

Furthermore, rabbit milk has potential applications in rabbit therapy and emotional support rabbit breeding. By developing rabbit milk-based products that promote relaxation and well-being, entrepreneurs in this niche can enhance the therapeutic benefits of their services.

Lastly, entrepreneurs involved in rabbit breeding and sales for laboratory research can explore the potential of rabbit milk as a research tool. By working with researchers and developing specialized rabbit milk formulas, they can contribute to advancements in various fields, such as nutrition and biomedical research.

In conclusion, developing and marketing rabbit milk specialty products offers a range of opportunities for entrepreneurs across different niches. By understanding the unique qualities of rabbit milk and tailoring products to meet the specific needs of their target markets, entrepreneurs can tap into this growing market and generate profits while contributing to the overall development of the rabbit industry.

Chapter 9: Rabbit Therapy and Emotional Support Rabbit Breeding

The Role of Rabbits in Therapy and Emotional Support

In recent years, rabbits have gained recognition for their incredible ability to provide therapeutic benefits and emotional support to individuals in need. This subchapter will explore the role of rabbits in therapy and emotional support, highlighting the potential opportunities for entrepreneurs in this field.

Therapy animals have long been used to promote healing and well-being in various settings, and rabbits have proven to be exceptionally effective in this regard. Their gentle nature, calming presence, and ability to form strong bonds with humans make them ideal candidates for providing emotional support. Whether it's in hospitals, nursing homes, schools, or even private homes, rabbits have shown tremendous potential in improving the lives of those struggling with physical, mental, or emotional challenges.

Entrepreneurs interested in breeding and selling rare rabbit breeds can tap into the growing demand for therapy rabbits. The demand for these specialized breeds, known for their calm temperament and therapeutic qualities, has been steadily increasing. By focusing on breeding and selling rabbits specifically for therapy purposes, entrepreneurs can cater to this niche market and provide a valuable service to individuals and institutions seeking therapy animals.

Additionally, entrepreneurs involved in rabbit pet breeding and sales can also explore the potential of breeding rabbits specifically for emotional support. Many individuals are turning to rabbits as emotional support animals due to their size, low maintenance, and compatibility with various living situations. By breeding rabbits with specific traits that make them well-suited for providing emotional support, entrepreneurs can meet the increasing demand for these unique companions.

Furthermore, entrepreneurs interested in promoting the use of rabbits in therapy can also explore partnerships with organizations and institutions that provide therapy services. Such partnerships can help raise awareness about the benefits of rabbits in therapy and create opportunities for collaboration and growth.

In conclusion, the role of rabbits in therapy and emotional support is a burgeoning field with immense potential for entrepreneurs. By focusing on breeding and selling rare rabbit breeds, or breeding rabbits specifically for therapy purposes, entrepreneurs can tap into a niche market and provide a valuable service to individuals and institutions seeking therapy animals. Furthermore, partnerships with therapy organizations can help promote the use of rabbits in therapy and create new opportunities for growth and collaboration.

Breeding and Training Rabbits for Therapy Purposes

Introduction:

Therapy animals have proven to be incredibly beneficial in improving mental, emotional, and even physical health. Among these therapy animals, rabbits have gained significant recognition for their gentle nature, intelligence, and adaptability. In this subchapter, we will explore the lucrative business opportunity of breeding and training rabbits specifically for therapy purposes.

Understanding the Demand:

The demand for therapy rabbits is rapidly increasing as more people recognize the positive impact these furry companions can have on their well-being. Entrepreneurs in the niche of breeding and selling rare rabbit breeds can tap into this market by selectively breeding rabbits known for their calm temperament, sociability, and compatibility with various environments.

Training Techniques:

Training therapy rabbits requires patience, consistency, and a deep understanding of the animal's natural behavior. Entrepreneurs interested in this niche can learn specialized training techniques such as clicker training, positive reinforcement, and desensitization exercises. These methods will help rabbits develop skills such as interacting with different individuals, responding to cues, and staying calm in various situations.

Certification and Licensing:

To ensure the credibility and professionalism of therapy rabbit breeding, entrepreneurs should consider obtaining necessary certifications and licenses. This step will help establish trust with potential buyers, including individuals seeking emotional support animals, therapists, hospitals, and assisted living facilities.

Collaborating with Therapists and Institutions:

Entrepreneurs in this field can form partnerships with therapists, mental health professionals, and institutions that incorporate animal-assisted therapy into their treatment programs. Collaborating with these professionals will not only expand the potential customer base but also provide valuable insights into the specific needs and requirements of therapy animals.

Marketing and Sales:

Effectively marketing therapy rabbits requires a comprehensive understanding of the target audience. Entrepreneurs can leverage social media platforms, create informative websites, and attend trade shows and conferences to showcase their rabbits. Additionally, offering personalized consultations and support to potential buyers will help establish long-term relationships and increase customer satisfaction.

Conclusion:

Breeding and training rabbits for therapy purposes presents a unique and profitable business opportunity. Entrepreneurs in this field can make a positive impact on people's lives while generating significant profits. By focusing on breeding rare rabbit breeds, mastering training techniques, obtaining necessary certifications, collaborating with therapists, and implementing effective marketing strategies, entrepreneurs can position themselves as leaders in the therapy rabbit industry.

Establishing Relationships with Therapy Organizations and Professionals

As an entrepreneur in the rabbit breeding industry, it is essential to establish strong relationships with therapy organizations and professionals. This subchapter will guide you on how to forge these connections to maximize your profits and contribute to the well-being of individuals who can benefit from the therapeutic effects of rabbits.

Therapy organizations and professionals play a crucial role in providing emotional support, comfort, and healing to people with various physical, mental, and emotional health conditions. Rabbits have been proven to be excellent therapy animals due to their gentle nature, ease of handling, and ability to form strong bonds with humans. By breeding and selling rabbits specifically for therapy purposes, you can tap into a niche market that is growing rapidly.

To start, research local therapy organizations in your area that cater to the specific niches you are targeting. Contact them to express your interest in collaborating and provide information about the unique rabbit breeds you offer. Highlight the qualities of your rabbits that make them suitable for therapy work, such as their calm temperament, intelligence, and adaptability.

Offer to organize visits or demonstrations at therapy centers, schools, or hospitals to showcase the benefits of rabbit therapy. This will allow therapy professionals to observe and interact with your rabbits firsthand, fostering trust and confidence in your breeding program.

Additionally, consider offering training workshops for therapy professionals who may want to incorporate rabbits into their programs. Provide educational materials on rabbit care, handling techniques, and the therapeutic benefits of rabbit-human interactions. This will position you as an expert in the field and help build credibility for your business.

Networking is also crucial in establishing relationships with therapy organizations and professionals. Attend conferences, workshops, and trade shows focused on therapy animals or related fields to connect with like-minded individuals. Exchange contact information and follow up with potential partners to explore collaboration opportunities.

Lastly, consider partnering with local veterinarians who specialize in therapy animals. They can provide valuable insights, guidance, and referrals to therapy organizations that are looking for reliable breeders.

By establishing relationships with therapy organizations and professionals, you can position yourself as a trusted source for therapy rabbits. This will not only benefit your business financially but also contribute to the well-being of individuals who can greatly benefit from the therapeutic effects of rabbits.

Chapter 10: Rabbit Breeding and Sales for Laboratory Research

Understanding the Demand for Laboratory Research Rabbits

In the world of rabbit breeding and sales, one niche that often goes unnoticed is the demand for laboratory research rabbits. These rabbits play a crucial role in scientific research and advancements in various fields, including medicine, genetics, and pharmaceuticals. As an entrepreneur in the rabbit breeding industry, it is essential to understand this niche and its potential for profits.

Laboratory research rabbits are specifically bred to meet the unique requirements of scientific experiments and studies. These rabbits are carefully selected for their genetic traits, health, and temperament, ensuring that they are suitable for various research purposes. Due to the specific needs of the scientific community, the demand for laboratory research rabbits remains consistently high.

One of the primary reasons why laboratory research rabbits are in demand is their genetic similarity to humans. Rabbits share many physiological and genetic traits with humans, making them ideal subjects for studying diseases, drug testing, and understanding various biological processes. Scientists rely on these rabbits to conduct experiments that can lead to groundbreaking discoveries and advancements in medical treatments.

Another reason for the demand in laboratory research rabbits is their reproductive capacity. These rabbits have been selectively bred to have high fertility rates, allowing researchers to have a sufficient number of subjects for their experiments. Additionally, their relatively short gestation period and fast growth rate make them an efficient choice for studies that require quick results.

Entrepreneurs who choose to specialize in breeding and selling laboratory research rabbits can tap into a lucrative market. Research institutions, pharmaceutical companies, and universities are always in need of high-quality rabbits for their studies. By understanding the specific requirements of these customers and providing rabbits that meet their criteria, you can establish yourself as a reliable supplier in this niche.

However, it is crucial to note that breeding and selling laboratory research rabbits come with unique challenges and ethical considerations. It is essential to ensure that the rabbits are treated with care and respect, and their welfare is a top priority. Maintaining high standards of hygiene, health, and proper housing conditions are essential for both the rabbits' well-being and the success of your business.

In conclusion, understanding the demand for laboratory research rabbits is vital for entrepreneurs in the rabbit breeding industry. By recognizing the unique needs of the scientific community and providing high-quality rabbits, you can tap into a profitable market. However, it is important to approach this niche with ethical considerations and prioritize the welfare of the rabbits. With the right approach, breeding and selling laboratory research rabbits can be a rewarding venture for both financial success and contributing to scientific advancements.

Meeting the Specific Requirements for Laboratory Rabbits

When it comes to breeding and selling rabbits for laboratory research, meeting specific requirements is crucial. Laboratory rabbits play a vital role in advancing scientific knowledge and finding cures for diseases. As an entrepreneur in this niche, it is essential to understand the unique needs and challenges associated with breeding and selling rabbits for this purpose.

First and foremost, laboratory rabbits must be bred and raised in a controlled environment. This includes maintaining strict hygiene standards to prevent contamination and the spread of diseases. Regular cleaning and disinfection of cages and equipment are essential to ensure the health and well-being of the rabbits.

Genetics also play a crucial role in laboratory rabbit breeding. Selecting rabbits with the desired traits, such as resistance to certain diseases or specific genetic markers, is important for research purposes. Collaborating with geneticists or experts in the field can help ensure that the rabbits you breed meet the specific requirements of research laboratories.

Another important aspect is providing appropriate nutrition and veterinary care to the rabbits. A balanced diet, rich in essential nutrients, is necessary to support their growth and overall health. Regular veterinary check-ups and vaccinations are essential to prevent the spread of diseases within the rabbit population.

Laboratory rabbits also need ample space for exercise and mental stimulation. Providing them with suitable enclosures or cages that allow for natural behaviors, such as hopping and digging, is crucial for their well-being. Enrichment activities, such as providing toys or tunnels, can help prevent boredom and promote their mental health.

Lastly, maintaining meticulous records is essential in the laboratory rabbit breeding business. Each rabbit should be properly identified, and detailed records of their genetic lineage, medical history, and research usage should be kept. This ensures traceability and accountability, which are important for compliance with regulatory standards.

Breeding and selling rabbits for laboratory research requires a deep understanding of the specific requirements and regulations in this niche. By meeting these requirements and providing high-quality rabbits, you can contribute to scientific advancements and make a positive impact in the field of medical research.

Building Partnerships with Research Institutions and Suppliers

In the world of pet breeding, establishing strong partnerships with research institutions and reliable suppliers can significantly enhance your success and profitability. Whether you specialize in breeding and selling rare rabbit breeds, raising rabbits for meat production, or any other niche within the rabbit industry, building these partnerships can provide invaluable opportunities for growth and expansion.

Research institutions play a crucial role in advancing the knowledge and understanding of rabbit genetics, health, and breeding techniques. By collaborating with these institutions, entrepreneurs in the rabbit breeding industry can access cutting-edge research, stay updated on the latest developments, and gain valuable insights into improving their breeding programs.

When establishing partnerships with research institutions, it is essential to foster open communication and collaboration. Attend conferences, seminars, and workshops organized by these institutions to network with experts and fellow breeders. Engage in conversations, share your experiences, and learn from others' successes and failures. By actively participating in these events, you can build relationships with researchers and establish yourself as a trusted partner in the industry.

In addition to research institutions, reliable suppliers are key players in the success of your rabbit breeding business. Suppliers provide essential resources such as quality feed, housing materials, breeding equipment, and veterinary supplies. Finding reputable suppliers who can consistently deliver high-quality products is crucial for ensuring the health and well-being of your rabbits, as well as maintaining the overall efficiency of your operation.

When selecting suppliers, prioritize those who understand the specific needs of your niche within the rabbit industry. For example, if you specialize in rabbit fur farming and selling pelts, seek suppliers who can provide you with the best grooming tools and fur care products. If your focus is on rabbit therapy and emotional support rabbit breeding, look for suppliers who offer specialized equipment and accessories to cater to this niche.

Establishing strong partnerships with research institutions and suppliers can also open doors to new markets and opportunities. Collaborating with researchers can lead to joint ventures, where you can share your expertise and contribute to groundbreaking studies. Working closely with suppliers can help you access exclusive products or negotiate better deals, giving you a competitive advantage in the market.

In conclusion, building partnerships with research institutions and suppliers is an essential aspect of running a successful rabbit breeding business. By collaborating with research institutions, you can stay at the forefront of industry advancements and gain valuable insights to improve your breeding programs. Reliable suppliers, on the other hand, ensure a steady supply of high-quality resources, contributing to the overall health and profitability of your operation. These partnerships not only enhance your business's reputation but also open doors to new markets and opportunities for growth and expansion.

Chapter 11: Rabbit Agility Training and Competitions

Exploring the World of Rabbit Agility

Rabbit agility training and competitions have gained significant popularity in recent years, attracting enthusiasts from various backgrounds, including entrepreneurs involved in different niches such as breeding and selling rare rabbit breeds, raising rabbits for meat production, rabbit fur farming and selling pelts, rabbit manure production for organic gardening, rabbit showmanship and competing in rabbit shows, rabbit pet breeding and sales, rabbit milk production for specialty products, rabbit therapy and emotional support rabbit breeding, and even rabbit breeding and sales for laboratory research.

In this subchapter, we will delve into the exciting world of rabbit agility and how it can open up new avenues for entrepreneurs in the rabbit industry. Rabbit agility is a sport that involves training rabbits to navigate through a series of obstacles, showcasing their agility, speed, and intelligence. It requires a deep understanding of rabbit behavior, training techniques, and patience.

Entrepreneurs involved in breeding and selling rare rabbit breeds can use agility training as a unique selling point for their rabbits. By showcasing the agility and trainability of their rabbits, breeders can attract potential buyers who are looking for rabbits that are not only visually appealing but also mentally and physically active.

For those in the rabbit pet breeding and sales niche, agility training can be a value-added service that sets their rabbits apart from others. Owners who are interested in participating in agility competitions or simply want a more active and engaging pet will be drawn to rabbits that have undergone agility training.

Moreover, rabbit therapy and emotional support rabbit breeding can benefit from agility training as well. These trained rabbits can provide mental and physical stimulation to individuals in need, helping them overcome anxiety or depression. Agility training not only enhances the rabbits' own well-being but also contributes to their ability to provide emotional support.

Entrepreneurs in other niches such as rabbit fur farming and selling pelts or raising rabbits for meat production can also explore agility training as a way to improve overall rabbit health and well-being. Engaging rabbits in physical activities can ensure they remain active and healthy, resulting in better-quality fur or meat.

In conclusion, rabbit agility training and competitions offer a unique opportunity for entrepreneurs in the rabbit industry to differentiate themselves from the competition and attract a diverse range of customers. Whether it is breeding and selling rare rabbit breeds, raising rabbits for various purposes, or engaging in therapy and emotional support rabbit breeding, agility training can benefit both the rabbits and the entrepreneurs involved. By exploring the world of rabbit agility, entrepreneurs can tap into a growing market and expand their business horizons.

Training and Preparing Rabbits for Agility Competitions

Agility competitions for rabbits have gained popularity in recent years, offering a unique and exciting way to showcase the athleticism and intelligence of our furry friends. Whether you are a seasoned entrepreneur in the rabbit industry or a newcomer looking for a profitable niche, understanding how to train and prepare rabbits for agility competitions can be a valuable skill to possess. In this subchapter, we will explore the key steps and techniques involved in preparing rabbits for these competitions.

The first step in training rabbits for agility competitions is selecting the right breed. While any breed can participate, certain breeds such as Dutch, Netherland Dwarf, and Mini Lop are known for their agility and quickness. Breeding and selling these rare rabbit breeds can be a lucrative venture for entrepreneurs looking to cater to the agility niche.

Once you have selected the right breed, it is essential to start training your rabbits from a young age. This helps them develop the necessary coordination and confidence to navigate the various obstacles in agility courses. Start with simple exercises such as jumping over hurdles and running through tunnels. Gradually increase the difficulty level as your rabbits progress.

Positive reinforcement is key to successful training. Use treats, praise, and clicker training to reward your rabbits for their accomplishments. This not only motivates them but also strengthens the bond between you and your rabbits. Consistency and patience are vital during the training process.

Creating a suitable training environment is also crucial. Set up a designated area with agility equipment such as jumps, tunnels, and weave poles. Make sure the area is safe and free from any potential hazards. Regular practice sessions will help your rabbits become familiar with the equipment and build confidence in their abilities.

In addition to training, proper nutrition and healthcare are essential for ensuring your rabbits are in optimal condition for competitions. Consult with a rabbit nutritionist to develop a diet plan that supports their energy needs. Regular veterinary check-ups and vaccinations are also necessary to prevent any health issues that may hinder their performance.

As an entrepreneur, you can capitalize on the growing popularity of rabbit agility competitions by offering training services, selling agility equipment, or organizing competitions and events. By understanding the training and preparation process, you can position yourself as an expert in the field and attract customers from various niches such as pet breeding and sales, therapy and emotional support rabbit breeding, and even laboratory research.

In conclusion, training and preparing rabbits for agility competitions can be a profitable venture for entrepreneurs in the rabbit industry. Selecting the right breed, starting training from a young age, using positive reinforcement, creating a suitable training environment, and ensuring proper nutrition and healthcare are the key steps to success. By mastering these techniques, you can tap into the growing market of agility competitions and provide valuable services to a wide range of niche markets within the rabbit industry.

Showcasing Agility Rabbits for Sale and Sponsorship Opportunities

Are you an entrepreneur looking to explore new and exciting opportunities in the world of rabbit breeding and sales? If so, this subchapter is just for you! In this section, we will delve into the fascinating world of showcasing agility rabbits and the various sponsorship opportunities that come with it.

Agility training for rabbits is a rapidly growing niche within the rabbit breeding industry. It involves training rabbits to navigate through obstacle courses, showcasing their speed, agility, and intelligence. Rabbit agility competitions have gained popularity among enthusiasts, attracting a large audience and potential customers.

For entrepreneurs interested in breeding and selling rare rabbit breeds, agility rabbits present a unique opportunity to tap into a niche market. These rabbits are in high demand among competitors and enthusiasts who are constantly seeking rabbits with exceptional agility skills. By showcasing and selling agility rabbits, you can cater to this specific market and command higher prices for your unique and talented rabbits.

Sponsorship opportunities within the agility rabbit industry are another avenue for entrepreneurs to explore. As the sport gains popularity, there is a growing need for sponsors to support competitions, events, and training programs. By becoming a sponsor, you can gain exposure for your breeding business and establish valuable connections within the industry. Sponsoring agility events can also provide you with a platform to showcase your rabbits and attract potential buyers.

In addition to breeding and selling agility rabbits, you can also consider offering training services to rabbit owners who are interested in getting their rabbits involved in agility competitions. By becoming an expert in agility training, you can position yourself as a valuable resource within the rabbit community and generate additional revenue streams.

As an entrepreneur, it is essential to stay ahead of the curve and identify emerging opportunities within your industry. Agility rabbits present a unique and exciting avenue to explore within the rabbit breeding and sales business. By showcasing your rabbits' agility skills and exploring sponsorship opportunities, you can tap into a niche market and establish yourself as a leader in the industry. So, why wait? Get ready to jump into the world of agility rabbits and unlock new possibilities for your business!

Chapter 12: Conclusion: Building a Profitable Rabbit Breeding Business

Recap of Key Strategies for Success

In the ever-evolving world of pet breeding and sales, it is crucial for entrepreneurs to stay ahead of the game and maximize their profits. This subchapter aims to recap some of the key strategies for success that have been discussed throughout this book, "Pet Breeding Profits: The Entrepreneur's Guide to Rabbit Sales," catering to various niches within the rabbit breeding industry.

1. Specialize in rare rabbit breeds: To stand out in the competitive market, consider breeding and selling rare rabbit breeds. By focusing on unique and sought-after varieties, you can attract customers who are willing to pay a premium for these exclusive pets.

2. Prioritize quality and health: Regardless of the niche you belong to, the quality and health of your rabbits should be your utmost priority. Regular check-ups, proper nutrition, and a clean living environment are essential for breeding healthy and thriving rabbits.

3. Build a strong network: Networking plays a vital role in any entrepreneurial venture. Connect with other breeders, suppliers, and industry experts to share knowledge, source high-quality breeding stock, and explore potential collaborations.

4. Market your products effectively: Develop a robust marketing strategy to reach your target audience effectively. Utilize online platforms, social media, and digital advertising to showcase your rare rabbit breeds, meat products, fur pelts, or any other niche-specific offerings.

5. Emphasize customer satisfaction: Whether you are breeding rabbits as pets, for meat production, or for any other purpose, ensure that your

customers receive exceptional service. Provide after-sales support, guidance, and care instructions to enhance customer satisfaction and build long-term relationships.

6. Stay updated with regulations: Depending on your niche, there may be specific regulations and guidelines to follow. Stay informed about animal welfare laws, breeding standards, and any other legal requirements to avoid any compliance issues.

7. Continuously educate yourself: The rabbit breeding industry is constantly evolving, and it's crucial to stay updated with the latest trends, breeding techniques, and market demands. Attend conferences, workshops, and seminars to expand your knowledge and improve your breeding practices.

Remember, success in the rabbit breeding industry requires passion, dedication, and a strong business acumen. By implementing these key strategies, you can position yourself as a leader in your chosen niche, whether it is breeding rare rabbit breeds, producing organic manure, participating in rabbit shows, or any other entrepreneurial endeavor within this diverse industry.

Resources and Tools for Further Growth and Expansion

As an entrepreneur in the field of pet breeding, there are numerous resources and tools available to help you grow and expand your business. Whether you are involved in breeding and selling rare rabbit breeds, raising rabbits for meat production, or any other niche within the rabbit industry, this subchapter will provide you with valuable information on the resources and tools that can support your success.

1. Expert Breeders and Associations: Connect with experienced rabbit breeders and join industry associations specific to your niche. These experts can provide guidance, share insights, and offer mentorship to help you improve your breeding techniques and expand your knowledge.

2. Online Communities and Forums: Engage in online communities and forums dedicated to rabbit breeding. These platforms allow you to connect with like-minded individuals, exchange ideas, and learn from others' experiences. Share your successes and challenges, and seek advice from fellow entrepreneurs.

3. Books and Publications: Stay updated with the latest industry trends and best practices by reading relevant books and publications. Look for resources that focus on your specific niche, such as books on rare rabbit breeds or meat rabbit production. These resources can provide valuable insights, tips, and strategies for success.

4. Educational Workshops and Conferences: Attend workshops, seminars, and conferences related to rabbit breeding. These events offer opportunities to learn from industry experts, gain practical knowledge, and network with other entrepreneurs. Stay informed about upcoming events through industry associations or online platforms.

5. Online Marketplaces and Platforms: Leverage online marketplaces and platforms to promote and sell your rabbit products. Platforms like Etsy, eBay, and specialized rabbit breeding websites can help you reach a wider audience and increase your sales potential.

6. Economic Development Programs: Explore economic development programs, grants, and funding opportunities that support small businesses in the rabbit industry. These resources can provide financial assistance for expansion, marketing, or research and development projects.

7. Veterinary Services: Establish a relationship with a reliable and experienced veterinarian who specializes in rabbits. Regular veterinary check-ups, vaccinations, and preventive care are essential for maintaining the health and well-being of your rabbits.

8. Technology and Software: Utilize technology and software tools to streamline your operations and improve efficiency. There are various software options available for managing breeding records, tracking sales, and analyzing business performance.

9. Marketing and Branding Strategies: Invest in marketing and branding strategies to promote your rabbit business. Develop a strong brand identity, create a professional website, engage in social media marketing, and explore advertising opportunities to reach your target audience.

10. Continuous Learning and Adaptation: Finally, remember that the rabbit industry is constantly evolving. Stay proactive by continuously learning, adapting to market trends, and exploring new opportunities for growth and expansion.

By utilizing these resources and tools, you can enhance your entrepreneurial journey in the rabbit breeding industry. Continuously seek knowledge, connect with experts, and embrace innovation to ensure the profitability and success of your business.

Inspiring Stories of Successful Rabbit Breeders-turned-Entrepreneurs

Introduction:

In the world of pet breeding, rabbit enthusiasts have found incredible success by turning their passion into profitable businesses. This subchapter explores the inspiring stories of rabbit breeders who have transitioned from hobbyists to successful entrepreneurs. Their experiences serve as valuable lessons for aspiring entrepreneurs in various niches, including breeding and selling rare rabbit breeds, raising rabbits for meat production, rabbit fur farming and selling pelts, rabbit manure production for organic gardening, rabbit showmanship and competing in rabbit shows, rabbit pet breeding and sales, rabbit milk production for specialty products, rabbit therapy and emotional support rabbit breeding, rabbit breeding and sales for laboratory research, and rabbit agility training and competitions.

1. Breeding and selling rare rabbit breeds:

Meet Sarah, a passionate rabbit breeder who recognized the demand for unique and rare rabbit breeds. Through extensive research and careful breeding, Sarah cultivated a collection of rare rabbit breeds, attracting customers from all over the world. Her success story highlights the importance of specialization and catering to niche markets.

2. Raising rabbits for meat production:

John, a former chef, combined his culinary skills with his love for rabbits to establish a successful rabbit meat production business. He educated customers about the nutritional benefits of rabbit meat and created a sustainable and ethical operation that appealed to health-conscious consumers.

3. Rabbit fur farming and selling pelts:

Emily's passion for sustainable fashion led her to start a rabbit fur farming business that prioritizes ethical practices. By providing high-quality pelts to fashion designers and artisans, she supports eco-friendly and cruelty-free fashion.

4. Rabbit manure production for organic gardening:

Mark recognized the potential of rabbit manure as a valuable organic fertilizer. He developed a system to collect and process rabbit waste, creating a profitable business that supplies organic gardens and farms with nutrient-rich compost.

5. Rabbit showmanship and competing in rabbit shows:

Linda's journey as a rabbit breeder started when she discovered the world of rabbit shows. Through dedicated training, meticulous grooming, and strategic breeding, Linda's rabbits consistently win top prizes at prestigious competitions. Her success story showcases the opportunities available in the competitive world of rabbit showmanship.

Conclusion:

These inspiring stories of successful rabbit breeders-turned-entrepreneurs demonstrate the vast potential within the diverse niches of rabbit breeding and sales. Whether it's catering to niche markets, capitalizing on sustainable practices, or excelling in competitive arenas, these entrepreneurs have found lucrative opportunities by turning their love for rabbits into profitable ventures. Aspiring entrepreneurs in these niches can learn valuable lessons from their experiences, enabling them to embark on their own paths to success.

www.ingramcontent.com/pod-product-compliance
Lightning Source LLC
Chambersburg PA
CBHW051305160726
47994CB00003B/1328

9 798223 784036